We are all different ages and sizes. We all have different coloured hair and skin. We are all good at different things.

Playing

When we play we can learn
new things.

When we play we can have fun.

When we play we can explore.

This man is using crutches to help him.

When we play we can exercise.

We can play many different sports.

How we play

Sometimes we play games with a ball.
Some people use a wheelchair to play.

Sometimes we build things when we play. People can build with sand on the beach.

Sometimes people play in a team.
This team is playing basketball.

Sometimes people play on their own.
This girl is blowing bubbles.

Sometimes people play with a partner. This girl is playing table tennis with a partner.

Sometimes people play in a club.
These children are playing
music together.

Sometimes people play computer games.

Sometimes people play with toys.

Where we play

Sometimes people play outside.

People play with skateboards outside.

Sometimes people play inside. Many people play music inside.

Children play at school. This girl is using a brace to help her play.

People play at home. These children
are playing in the garden.

We are all different

There are many different ways of playing. Which do you like best?

Words to know

brace something people wear to help them grow and move

crutches long poles that some people use to walk

wheelchair chair with wheels. Some people use wheelchairs to get around and play sport.

Index

Note to parents and teachers

Before reading
Encourage the children to think of the ways that they are different from one another. Then explain that being different makes everyone special. Ask the children to form pairs. Ask them to talk to a partner and to tell each other their favourite game. Then ask each partner to tell you what their partner likes to play. Collect in the answers and list them under sports, board games, music, computer games, and playground games on the board.

After reading
Tell the children to look through magazines and catalogues and to cut out pictures of people playing sports, music, or games. Make a collage of these pictures and help the children to write labels for each activity. Then lead children in a discussion about the many ways that people can play.